# POEMS, MAXIMS AND TALES

Marc Savett

NFB
Buffalo, New York

ISBN: 978-0692597279
Poems, Maxims, and Taele/Savett-1st ed.

1. Poems. 2. Maxims. 3. Tales.

4. Verse. 5. Fiction 6.

Cover and back photographs courtesy of the author

No Frills Buffalo/Amelia Press
<<<>>>
119 Dorchester Road
Buffalo, New York 14213
For more information please visit
nofrillsbuffalo.com

Thank you Noah, Wendy and Kathleen Anderson.

I ran a few marathons of writing into
Poems,Maxims, and Tales.

# CONTENTS

## THE POEMS

HE GRIPS WITH BOTH HANDS                        8
SLEEP WALKER                                    9
THE BENEFACTOR                                  10
DEATH OF ANTINOUS C.100-130                     11
FOOLS GOLD                                      12
DESERT NOIR                                     13
SONDER KOMMANDOS                                14
THE LOTTERY                                     15
TRANE TIME – WEBERS MIDDLETOWN 1958             16
FLOATING                                        17
THE APPOINTMENT                                 19
THE PLATOON WAS SHOOTING                        20
JAMES STREET BLIGHT                             21
SACRIFICE TO THE MASTERS                        22
PORTRAIT OF D. H. KAHNWEILER                    23
A BIRD WITH SHRILL SONG                         24
PAST INDISCRETIONS                              25
OH BEAUTY                                       26
NUTRITIVE ABSENCE REVISED                       28
HE WAS LYING COMFORTABLY                        29
PRINCES AND FROGS                               30
SWIMMING POOL                                   31
BEFOULED BY A SHREW                             32
PASSION SONG                                    33
GREEK PUNTER                                    34
BUFFALO DETOUR                                  35
FIEDLER'S GAZE                                  36
CRUEL CUTLASS                                   37
DE CHEVAL                                       38
CLOCKWORKS                                      39
CAVE DANCE                                      41
A CARD GAME                                     42
50'S CHEVY HATCHING THE FUTURE                  44

HE HEARD A BABY CRYING    46
JADED MANTRAS    47
ZIHUATANEJO    48
MOON DOG    49
ALCHEMY – PALMER SHAFT    50
ANTS PASSION    51
AUTUMN #25    52
DYLAN TAPE    53
GUNSLINGER    55
HE SMELLED EXOTIC SPICES    56

## THE MAXIMS

THE SENTENCE AND THE PERIOD    58
THE EARTHWORM AND THE GROUNDHOG    59
THE HAWK AND THE FARMBOY    60
THE PORCUPINE AND THE GADFLY    61
THE RAVEN AND THE VULTURE    63
THE ROSE AND THE FEVERFEW    65
THE SKUNK AND THE DUCK    66
THE WILDEBEEST AND THE LION    67
BLINDNESS ON THE ROAD    68
MAGNIFICENT SPECIMENS    69
FROGS ASCENDENCE    70
CHIPMUNK'S CHATTER    71
THE OVERZEALOUS MEN AND THE WISEMEN    72

## THE TALES

CEPHALOPODS    74
JOHN RAMSEY    77
THE WOODEN BOX    82
CARMEN    86
WALL OF LEARNING    90
THE STACKER    91

# THE POEMS

### HE GRIPS WITH BOTH HANDS

He grips both hands on the bottom rung
Of a rope ladder
How did he arrive at this point?
He refuses to let go
Feeling the void below
Ready to snap him up in its geophysical jaws
A nurse appears at his bedside

Though he never put much stock in magic
He enjoyed joking and laughing with her
This was contagious
He needed her company
Which she freely gave him
There were campfires in the night
He chased an army before him

Some were screaming orders;
Others moaning from their wounds
She asked him if he wanted to play chess
He declined stating that the pieces
Have grown heavy

Particularly the queen and king
He fell into sleep
Dreaming of painting along the spacious hallways
She left a note for him
Saying that she had shared his dreamscape
As he awoke to a sliver
Of waning moon sinking

## SLEEP WALKER

I am a poor sleeper. My father and grandfather before him
Were light in sleep though a catnap in a backroom made up
The deficit. Irritability was part or our character. Bears
Growling day and night in our den.

Then my life deteriorated  into sleep states lost in my own
Room. I was a sleep walker zombied smashing into dressers
Lost in the constricting corridors around my bed dragging
One foot after another crawling over obstacles disoriented

To position groveling through bed covers pounding on closets
Caught in a hypnotic knot begging for the salvation of wakefulness
With haunted eyes mouldering in darkness lost in dark spells
Dreamscapes and madness

## THE BENEFACTOR

At first they seemed exotic beings
Not of this world but extraterrestrials
Complexions creamy sunsets
There- after another side of personality
Surfaces quickly settling into new surroundings

Unpredictable dangerous blasphemies
Households infested with parasites rodents
And snakes acting as if a fourth party in the
Room is their benefactor

Living a lifetime in fogs obligations to land
And homestead as the pendulums curse sizes
The owner with each stroke becoming guardians
Of worms and filth while putrescence and insects wait

Running is not possible with this much glue on our feet
The benefactor gives permission to gift the family
Beyond the grave for nailing the coffin
Then throwing the ashes into eternity

## DEATH OF ANTINOUS C.100-130

The Emperor of the world Hadrian set sail with a flotilla of boats
His crew sailed the vessel into a stiff head wind on an unpredictable river
Moving pottery gold scarabs lamps and hippopotamus teeth as the sky grew
Into blackness the Nile waters raged. The young man Antinous was thrown
Off the prow into a maelstrom of question as crocodiles snapped their jowls on
the surface

His face revealed impeccable mathematic symmetry
Beauty admired by kings queens emperors and gods
In death statuesque with a face like marble cold to the touch
Hadrians favorite bloom merged into the others love platonically

The Emperor deified his beloved and constant companion. Antinous was
To celebrate the festival of Osiris prior to his demise perhaps poisoned by
A jealous suitor or cursed by a magic potion on the mystical river Nile
Others poured over Dynastic texts searching for solutions though
Unable to break curses and paradox while in time coins minted
Display Antinous in bas-relief

**FOOLS GOLD**

They were intimate charmed with the other
Intoxicated in the smoke like some
Holy book with its thick incantations a wall
Impervious to all incursions solemn

Crossing invisible boundaries where fish
Jump high in tranquil waters through the seasons
As if nothing existed but our hearts
Fragile glass through existential necessities

Finally caught love and desire by the tail
Swung three times round before they slapped
Their sides laughing like fools silly as they
Fell to the ground eyes tears and lovers still

## DESERT NOIR

We are photographs that must not be appropriated
From walls though they hang flawed
The images narrate a fragile noir unfolding
The climax in jagged detours with guns pointed
To the desert cracking through betrayal
She stares at a muscular lover lost in a bubble
Of anxiety as they hum melancholic anthems inside respective
Frames while lovers purr through an atmosphere

Of fog and mist as illusion hides within deception's
Embrace there is the looking back farewell
Swallowed by eyes regret changing hue
Falling through background greys to silence
As a gold tooth becomes a beacon searching for the apocalypse
Prospectors are lost in darkness back lit
By fifth degree light finding meaning in
Broken dreams drama and desert night

## SONDER KOMMANDOS

Sonder Kommando Jews were assigned by nazis
To dispose of their own into the crematoriums
After the Zyklon B gas smashed the travelers
Into a tidal wave of twisted humanity

They counted the heads
Then dug deep from memory
Where they last observed the buried
The instability of the chest wall
Crumbling from the weight
Squeezing breath from the most powerful
Sonder Kommandos collecting jewels and treasure

After the families, tricked into a final trip
In boxcars, journeying through hell
Without luxury of food or drink
Pied pipers lead the hordes
Midst insane dogs barking
To the showers where sweet music
Plays on smiles as the pellets drop

## THE LOTTERY

Life seemed bland when suddenly
Gold and rare gems fell from the heavens
He was swimming in strange seas of plenty
After days of celebration,
He dreamed his extremities were bound
By a frightening hook and pulley system
That stretched his mouth to a scream

The next morning the commute
Became a slide down a death chute
He was driving anxiously through a dark tunnel
Full of high beams, projectiles of tractor-trailers
SUV's and large beasts sharing the road
His path a toboggan run of rain ice snow and fog

Every day became an insecure adventure
On rough seas he strapped on his seatbelt at six am
He felt his state change from solid to liquid mercury
Disappearing through his fingers
The celestial bounty falling through lullaby's lost luster

Exhilaration was recast a sickness in the gut
The good fortune became a lottery of drives
Through thick danger morning and night
He felt that he had swallowed poison
Rather than heavenly manna

He was a shadow running with shadows
A creature flying through darkness
Scampering down tunnels even at midday
Angst for the twilight chained to gold and the night

**TRANE TIME – WEBERS MIDDLETOWN 1958**

The earth a shuttering rumble
Trembling intensifying
Train horn cutting morning light
The massive grey-black behemoth diesel engine
Makes a slow wide turn with Cyclops beam
As clouds of steam envelop the train

Racing autos try to beat the black and white gates
The red-flashing signal with loud staccato bell
Ringing frantically
Pedestrians running a death-course across the tracks

A bullet of engine-song exploding past
Slowing sliding through the steam
Stopping at the Middletown red brick station
Commuters in black suits and shoes
White shirts fedoras rush to board
Brakes screech as the train builds momentum
Toward N.Y.C.

## FLOATING

The Buffalo station alerted listeners
That there was a body
Floating lazily down Riverside Canal
Yes, it was dead, according to sources
I felt sure it was my double
Personifying  ennui hovering about
Floating gently down a placid canal
The sharp beaked birds peck at my flanks
Foraging for insects
This would be annoying
If it were not for the sound of distant rapids
Culminating in a foamy collage
Dropping over the landmark Horseshoe Falls

I feel the adrenaline pump
Then a pulse of endorphins
Palliating discomfort and pain
But I look skyward from the perspective
Of my nakedness exposed to a yellow sun
Traveling where soft currents take me
Away from the complexities of entanglements
With their misunderstandings
That float through my dreams
They interface with the elixir of deep REM sleep
That may have led to the naked back float
Down turgid cool waters in early summer
No gunshot wound or poisonous substance

Only a thick unhappiness
From the constant drip of boredom
Consuming a stream of options
Part of the nightly queue
Ping-ponging my mind
Until you pull the lever

Feeling a wall of eyes watching
From the riverbank
Twisted in self consciousness
What is real is the staring
At my story
Which floats before me
I can hear them whisper

Chatting uncomfortably
Though this is quite faint
Really just another day
A Buffalo radio news flash
Noted that a naked man
Was floating down
The Riverside Canal
Defiled with oil, gas, and algae

## THE APPOINTMENT

We are in the waiting room. Our appointments are imminent
There is squirming finger tapping. Men scratch rhymically jiggling
Their lower legs. The heart jumps in the chest. The stomach speaks
In gurgles and low frequency rumbles. There is discomfort. Some
Message their heads.  They all are in the same boat rocking in shallow
Water. Some behave as if they are sea sick holding their stomachs
Each in their seat wondering what the others affliction might be
Eyes trying not to be obvious each interested in the others diagnosis.

Ferreting out what significance a cough or sneeze might hold. They all have
Appointments some waiting for two hours. Patients seem paralyzed in fear
And anger though they continue to sit waiting their turn as the doctor attired
in A sports jacket opens the door sending a spasm through the crowd anxious
For direction. Some smile artificially others shutter. An older women cries
Softly while all remain resigned to wait as several begin to converse.
The doctor stands at the window writing a prescription

## THE PLATOON WAS SHOOTING

The platoon was shooting machine guns
Popping sounds splitting air
Chasing warriors with turbans
Explosions tore the mountain
Gunfire was exchanged
He awoke hyperventilating
On the queen size bed

Above him the pink boulder
Below death
Tears fell from his cheeks
He was floating toward the horizon
Ready for his ultimate battle
Tired looking toward the boulder
Above him he prayed it might roll off
Its unstable perch
Onto his lap

## JAMES STREET BLIGHT

My grandparents were immigrants from Eastern Europe
They immigrated to the United States in the early twentieth century
Through Ellis Island
Moving to James Street
Melting pot for enterprising
Italians, Polish, Greeks and Jews.

There is a string of ghettos across New York State
Amidst pockets of wholeness there exists an underbelly of corruption
Ransacked houses populated by addicts and junkies
Shootings murders and arson are the landscape

Like large pieces of meat rotting from the inside out
There are nightly skirmishes body bags floating toward the grave
City fathers have complicated agendas
Limited funding and short memories

The tailor shop has been devoured by ghetto
It feels dangerous
Windows shattered
Bright red graffiti on yellow clapboard
Across the face of the old tailor shop
Once infused with the smells of freshly pressed suits

## SACRIFICE TO THE MASTERS

The models sit motionless on soft leather benches
In the echoing halls of the museum
They imagine themselves in the artist's studio
Holding limbs in asymmetrical geometries
Posing naked before the master
Staring at photographs of violins and bulls
On the wall

Tight breasts and a delicate triangle of red hair
Below the navel is a box of truffles
Devoured by the painter
They believe the master is fixated on them
With Van Gogh eyes
They daydream of being the subject
Of an important work
With their skirts and jeans falling away
Into a bluish-yellow wash of landscape
Under a hot sun

Youth is a sweet treasure
To be caressed and then swallowed
As blonde hair flows down a blouse
Caught in perfect proportion
Frozen in a frame of time

There are busty women and satyrs
Running through dreamy forests
With flushed cheeks and pubescent urges
Their lips are wet and succulent
As a dripping peach
They are full of tension
As the artist covers the canvass
With brush strokes dipped in deep pigments
Applied tenderly to soft faces
Longing to be touched

## PORTRAIT OF D. H. KAHNWEILER

He is a reflection on puffs of fog
His portrait lies within diffuse planes of soft light
Chameleon eyes dart from the angles
Of isosceles triangles, wisps of his face
Float toward the skylight
Picasso deconstructs D.H.
With deft brushstrokes

The structure on canvas shifts shape
Casting gray shadow as nimbus cumulus clouds
Inspire and expire their breath
He wears a deep misty mask
Reflected as rectangles multiplying
To infinity across the ponds of the mind

He stands buoyant as a hot air balloon
With a hundred faces built from molecules in motion
The painter throws his vapors toward the canvas
Intoxicating as scotch over ice
A mystery dressed in gray revealing little

### A BIRD WITH SHRILL SONG

He flew  down riverbeds with the bird
Then up the walls of sleep
Then down canyons
Until he fell from the dream
Waking in a puddle of sweat
In the queen size bed
He had dreamed of walking through

Rooms of oil paintings
Lost in their frames
With the flying figures of Chagall
There was the reverie
Of all he had seen and touched
He placed his collections on shelve
In a private space
His vision explored each piece
She stood before him
As he awoke from a deep sleep

## PAST INDISCRETIONS

He waited for my sleep
Wanting no resistance
He was a creature placed in my room
Vengeance for past crimes
Crawling ever closer
To test my strength, my impotence

I sensed he would come
For the past forgets few indiscretions
Shadows of fire are sent
To engulf the forgetful
I suddenly awake from a deep sleep
Reaching for my thigh

My body tightened
Apparitions flashing the
Name of my wickedness
Fly like bats through my body
My right leg swells
A chill shook me

I fought the creatures
Deceptive stratagems
Finding the tarantula
I kill him with a shoe
I know more are coming
It will not end.

## OH BEAUTY

The young deconstruct themselves
Caterpillars tearing off incarnations
Rarely comfortable with their new faces
Centipede mouth or bird eyes
They are in tumult
Swarming in volcanoes
They remake self-hate and loathing
Into an industry

They are confused by their address
They face death continuously
Driving recklessness to the limit
They live in accidents
Imaginings of rivals
Ride on tracks of jealousy
Leading to disillusion and trite rewards

They're mesmerized by the reflection
On the surface of their stream
Their emotions are blown glass
They do their dance as bees
Before they fly from the hive
Seeking the nectar of life
They are birds-of-paradise
Puffing out feathers

Anointed beautiful
They are eventually cracked by time
Doubt is a nervous bedfellow
A facial convexity
Shadowing a concavity of spirit
Vanity is the scrap yard of insecure youth
Congregations of the young serve as oracles
That buoys the wounds of imperfection
And asymmetry

Friends fill them with oxygen
The petty conceits of childhood
Are gobbled up by the frantic pace of life
Detritus blowing back behind
They fly into their pursuits
Leaving self consciousness in its wake
While superficiality moans its swan song

## NUTRITIVE ABSENCE REVISED

If something went awry
I would wither with you
For we are of the same soil
We thrive on the same vital nutrients
The clear water that kisses my brain
Embraces yours

We are sparrow hawks that push
Against the high air in synchrony
Our gods are of the earth
We are beholden to those
Who have moved humanity
In small steps forward

We play in each other's language
As effortlessly as hummingbirds climb
And swoop invisible half-pipes
When we part
I miss your presence which is mine
You become a hologram in front of me
That is disembodied
I push my hand through you
Without ever touching you
It is then I feel my emptiness
Without you

## HE WAS LYING COMFORTABLY

He was lying quietly under the pink boulder
Death in his long robes floated past
As he was daydreaming of his rendezvous
With his secretary
He could see her black hair
Falling down her back
As a candle flickered on the table
As he was touching the tail end of a dream
Over him hung the pink boulder
Protecting but simultaneously threatening

With the potential of collapse
As a cliff falls into the sea
With the weight of the world on his head
He looked in a mirror
His gaze ricocheting off his retinas
He walked through the door
Setting the security alarm
He sat with her at the pub
Ordering martinis before he realized
He was sleeping comfortably
Below the pink boulder

## PRINCES AND FROGS

Narcissism blooms with the perfumed essence
Of estrogen and testosterone
Flexing muscles and feminine seductions
The buxom blonde teacher pulls
A large frog from creation's soup

To observe and then dissect the anatomy
As the spring sun warm shimmering in hot hormones
Reflected in themselves
Life forms primitive or complex
Journeying with the planet

Sharing dreams and breathing the atmosphere
Secretions that procreate the substance of life
Perplexed by mystery permeating the young men and women
Embarrassed by considering the moment of conception
Obsessed with its raging desires and secret fires

Enlightened by a teacher's lamp that streams facts
Explaining life with the atoms that sing of love
Swimming in fluids as frogs in a pond
Life lived in a composition of hydrogen
Oxygen and nitrogen invisibly essential

Inverted roles where princes become frogs
A noir on screen acted before an audience
Fished from casks as the first amphibians
Climbed from the salty brine
Students pulling themselves into their future

## SWIMMING POOL

At six years the boy dove into a pool that appeared deep
As the heavens, though was but three feet shallow
Slamming his head on the bottom he recalled
Strange lobsters that chattered like sparrows
Enormous worms with fins like a dolphin tickled his nose
Blue fish circled his body singing phrases of nursery rhyme

The sun's rays covered the boy with white light while
Drifting toward the surface taking his first
Explosive breath as all below disappeared he
Recalled the strange creatures he had met as he awakened
From a deep sleep his head lying on a pillow though
No one believed his journey since no one had witnessed
His fine dive before resting quietly on the pool bottom

**BEFOULED BY A SHREW**

The shrew is gifted from the principle gods
Who fume with jealousy when the minor gods experience
Bliss. This female is a tough customer with a loathsome
Disposition and scorching temperament.

A perfect concoction of beauty spouting venom and blasphemies
Toward her competition. Her tongue a drill bit that courses
Through the unwary. Beauty splatters perfume and acid
On her enemies. She is befouled by compounds of witches

Brew dangerous watching porno on the flat screen holding
A cell phone while calling uncles and lovers. The enchantress
Flashes her saber like nails. Her basement is filled with rows of
Skeletons that sway to Bartok's String Concerto

The shrew cannot control her hawk like screams an unmuzzled
Banshee haunted with paranoia and drug shelf dreams.
She is fragile living through broken covenants and betrayals
Deceptive visions of reality turn revenge into her parlor game

**PASSION SONG**

Snakes soaking up heat in the grass. All life forms reborn
In the early rains. Every organism restored for another
Year hydrogen furnaces of sun stoked. Fawns with their
Blankets of spots cavorting with gambols high intoxicated
With the lilies of the valley, purple hyacinths, tulip and crocus
Frozen in potential after heavy north country winter
Now in late April exploding with life baby mammals drunk on
Thick smells of earth covering nakedness with luxuriant

Leaf growth midst endless shades of green tapestry in myriad
Forms. Symphonies of tree frog peeper and bird
Song. Warblers yellow black and orange cover the pine
Branches candelabra primrose daffodils and iris fill the
Creeks with blooms wood duck and mallards find the
Pond season after season, beavers dam.  Bees
Pollinate all variety and color of wild flower. Bears
Break their long hibernation. Life percolates upward.

**GREEK PUNTER**

He aspired to throw the discus posing like
Like a Greek god wound tight then exploding
With torque as the disk flew over the soggy ground

Leaves fell as he punted a football for hours
Imagining it tumbling inside the five yard line
His arms never long enough for the discus

Legs too short to punt prodigious distances
Though disappointed with short comings
He became more realistic toward achieving
The possible ignoring goals wasted on the
Improbable.

## BUFFALO DETOUR

There she was on the jet diverted to Buffalo
Breathing oxygen from drop down air masks
Experiencing a rapid loss of cabin pressure
Losing altitude thousands of feet per minute semi conscious

Thinking of existence and the ease of being
Plucked like a daffodil from this life by brute
Force crossing repetitious routine
Knocked unconscious flying in formation

With migratory birds while people come
And go first cries and final exhalations
Never anxious to make a splash in the obituaries
Only longing for a last voyage through the

End of time with a lover arm and arm
Under April showers as long as the future
Lasts in the by and by now lost in springtides
Early fragrances

Feeling romance immersed in warm breezes
Lifting the weary far from early winters
Crushing ironies caught in a net of bird song
Growing feathers taking flight

## FIEDLER'S GAZE

Fiedler wrote letters to Philip
Who lived with Susan
Near Fordham in the Bronx
One describing two hundred year old letters
From an obscure Franciscan monk
Bound in red leather on shelves of the
Bibliotheque de la Sorbonne
Philip had just completed an independent study in Wales
He replied to Leslie with a Haiku
A shrimp floating through octopus ink
Overwhelmed in blackness looks backward
Philip was obsessed with a woman who lived
In a third floor apartment who skied with him in the Alps
It was ten degrees on a February morning
As he emerged from the subway after landing at Kennedy
Strolling down the grand concourse with a backpack
Breath steaming from his mouth
Collapsing on a bed with Susan
Watching commuters down the hill
Amorphous through the vapors and dust
He envisioned Fiedler's furrowed brow

## CRUEL CUTLASS

Crisscrossed hearts pine in remorse's wake
They cry a forlorn refrain
Requiem for great deeds long forsaken
Wrecked onshore and battlefield bitter
What has been said and done is spent
A bronze soldier cannot act
An old drum runs through by cruel cutlass
Sharpened only now for future reckonings

## DE CHEVAL

The French officer De Cheval
Rides through heated battle
Slashing the sky to fragments
Those float down to the killing field

A Spanish lieutenant lies mortally wounded
His blood awash on the earth
Passion for duty drives soldiers
To defend homestead and lovers

The queen's castle
Lifts its musket,
Toppling the black king
Who jumps off the chess board

Holding the magic box of devotion
In their hearts
Duty drives the will of ten thousand
Soldiers into battle

Inflexible allegiance binds their intentions
To symbolic chimeras of their birthright
Rigid faith if not questioned
Is dreamland?
That slips off clouds into regret
Of strategies not considered

If one's true conviction
Is not freed from its cage
An officer's creativity
May fall on his own sword
As the fire of war rages
And a tear falls
From De Cheval's eye

## CLOCKWORKS

Never at ease with the image she projected
On the walls of her truncated world
All her self-hate was forgotten
When lost in work

Her insides were wheels, spindles and springs
Her inner works functioned with the precision of a Rolex
She would batten down in her office
Lost in protocols policies and regulations
Her charges were held to her compulsive standards
She memorized the black book
Fifteen hundred pages of policy and legalese

Though her recitations were faultless
She felt naked in front of her superiors
Her watch works at those times giving her indigestion
Her confidence hung tacked to a corkboard
Hundreds of pages in her mind that reassured her intentions
With the officers of command
She became lost in application of the black book
She pushed harder to recall policy
Though froze mixing policies like Martinis

It seemed she was now in her office for hours
Subordinates could hear muttering
As if she were reading Shakespearean sonnets
For hours on end
Her staff wondered if they were imagining wheels in place of eyes
A winding mechanism where her mouth sat
They would hear chimes and ticks
That seemed to emanate from her head
She started to quote obscure regulations wildly

Sending out warnings

Of severe consequences to staff
If they violated her obscure tenants
Her dictates changed by the hour
One crisscrossed another until
All sanity was tied in a knot
For several days she could not be located
They found her in a deep trance unable to speak intelligibly
But for reciting policy and regulations in no sensible order

*C*

## CAVE DANCE

The anthropologist is a magician
A conjuror of spirits who speak for the dead
Fleshing out relationships inside a DNA strand
Recreating tongues to express the affections of those gone
Mere bone chips discovered in remote caverns
Redefine life from millenniums past
Allowing the living to speculate reverberated words
Echoing off rock walls articulated from distant lips
Mixing syllable to sound
Capturing the essence of the ancients

The scientist feels commonality through their potential
To envision DNA of Neolithic man in Homo sapiens
Deciphering genes in pottery and bones
Solving puzzles of a saber tooth embedded in a skull bone
Codes in genes that paint a vocabulary of ancient man
Exposing Twitter man to his past
Rock engravings 10,000 BC
Cave painting Lascaux 15,000 BC
Lyrical documentary on bear cave walls
Ancient prehistoric communities revealed
Early man is carbon dated

## A CARD GAME

He was becoming forgetful depression
And senility getting the best of him
He frequently would say
That life was tenuous

The existentialist provided staples for his family
Food, a roof over his kids' head,
That felt as secure as a sailboat
Moored tightly to the dock
Rheumatic fever was a time bomb
Waiting to explode his heart
Which it did one morning

At work, it struck hard
When I answered the call
Informing me of his death
How can immortal gods die?
The clear evidence was
His heart was pumping at thirty-five percent
He thought the walls in his room were streaked
With a mysterious yellow poison
That was killing him

The psychiatrist prescribed medication
That could calm his tumultuous nature
Though at times I think a medical approach
Could never have been powerful enough
There could only be a more radical departure

Like a big-stakes card game
Poker or gin rummy
He in his seersucker suit, loafers,
With thousands in chips on the table
And three buxom ladies staring over his shoulder
This would have brought him back to life

Then a quick trip to the flat track
Would have probably rescued his heart
And given him six more months

## 50'S CHEVY HATCHING THE FUTURE

She took the signature of the moon
Derivative of the giant green Luna moth
Four eyes patterned over silky wings
Cultivator of gardens
Queen of poppies sage tulips and hyacinths
Moon goddess of dance
Priestess of lunacy
Dionysian lover of nature and excess
Butterflies landing on her shoulders
Sipping out of her wine glass

Master of panic paralyzed by phallic snakes
Slithering through her rock piles
Screaming hysterical as she ran backwards
From her own fruit
Those in her gravity
Could only run asunder
To save the ends and beginnings of themselves
Those children of the moon
Drank her silk moth potions
Becoming glazed-eyed nectar intoxicated

They cloistered in bunkers of solitude
To take back their future
To preserve a piece of themselves
Smoking vines in the back seat
Of a wrecked 50's Chevy
With an arm around a
Prepubescent girlfriend
Field grass growing over the roofline
Chewing wild rhubarb
That exploded like kisses
And ambrosia in their mouths

Making dates with eternity
Summer cherry light
Falling on the future
In the rumble seat of the 50's Chevy

## HE HEARD A BABY CRYING

He dreamed of rattlesnakes in battle
Under the pink boulder
He felt a palpable danger
As the snakes whipped their tails
In secret code
As mortal enemies fought

And the network sparked
Like a severed wire
Then the flood of snakes
Overwhelmed him
As they crawled from behind his eyes
As he watched the movie
Playing devious tricks with his fear
He fell through the enigma
Into the deepest satisfying sleep

## JADED MANTRAS

We carry shards of experience mirrors reflecting
Beauty and venom Greek drama in chorus
Singing cures for frailty of the spirit
There are short sojourns in rest homes to change the oil

Ferrari's graze on petrol saturating the soil with putrescence
Jaded mantras sung by an enchantress who lost her compass
Viewing an old photo of Madame Curie spilling a shot glass
Of radioactivity

Three men sit round the table watching chess pieces dance
Mental is less physical there is only the Syrian crossroads
Playground for soldiers of fortune run through by foreign
 Invaders that fight crooked wars where exquisite treasure is

Sledge hammered to elemental atoms the young rotting devoured
By monsters wearing masks hoods eye liner pigtails and epaulets
They sail seas of filth fish entangled in plastic while God
Recedes from humanities cataclysms beasts feed off his reputation

### ZIHUATANEJO

Excursion to the Mexican coast
Driving deep green rain forest
Jaguar eyes follow the progression
The driver played with fate
Careening down a river bank
Saved by a one inch bough
Locals pushed the VW back on the dirt road
The beach is white sand
Coconut palms and blue light
Three tents in place secured
Eating rice beans and chicken
Looking into the eternity of the Pacific
In darkness swimming naked in the pink and blue swirls
Of phosphorescence

The next morning flipping in waves
Crashing head on the sandy bottom
Floating to the surface neck numb
Moving arms and legs
Laying on white sand dazed by tingling bolts of electricity
Thinking how moments can change tomorrows
Cursing surfing gods
Thanking lady luck for dodging paralysis
Crossing a beach crawling with scorpions
Thankful for a reprieve from a prison of desolation
My fragile connection with existence
Narrowly missing tragedy
Watching an octopus glide back and forth
Over the coral before disappearing

## MOON DOG

The furry black and white malamute ran in circles
The entire night trying to crack the puzzle of
Moonlight this milky reflection of sunlight hanging
Stolid while snow pellets sparkled like a billion
Motes bursting in colors through a crystal prism
Driving the dog to howl and lunge at the object
Above jittery untouched by human hands
Or the dog's aggressive barks and whining

A mysterious sphere the dog scared of its own
Crunchy footsteps that he attributes to the annoyance
Above him an eye staring down in the harsh night angered
That he can't jump to it like a leap to a boulder
The moon appearing close sitting on her throne 240,000
Miles from earth angered by her intrusiveness
The brashness of the beam covering blackness with
With light the malamute unable to grip the object above
On the tether with its snapping jaws

## ALCHEMY – PALMER SHAFT

Mines hold the worth of the nation
They are deep pits magical with strange alchemies
Skyscrapers rise out of their ore
Miners work in tight spaces
Constricting tunnels that take the breath
The potential of being sucked down a shaft
Falling through the grizzly to the ore crusher
Is a beast staring the miner in the eyes
Senses must be acute to dodge a timber pole
Busting loose rattling its way down a shaft
Blowing through anything in its path
Nitroglycerin explosions blast ore from the stoops
Giving men splitting headaches and nasty dispositions
As ore is melted to pure metal
A man's substance is transformed
Working the bowels of the earth

Miners have first dibs on exceptional specimens they find
Collectors covet the spectacular material
Avarice consumes the serious collector
If there are only thirty rocks that fluoresce a sizzling orange
In the world
Ownership can be a shot of opium in the brain
A man who believes his buddies are mining in his lunchbox
Has lost his compass
A collector can buy a "killer specimen"
And have his pocket picked by the seller simultaneously
He then feels like he is in free fall
A thousand feet down the Palmer Shaft
At that instant the alchemy is complete.

## ANTS PASSION

There was a glorious passion flower vine
On my chain link fence when I lived in Mexico
Green leaves covered the links
The blooms were numerous
Large as sunflowers, purple and white
With a waxy quality reflecting the morning sun

They were the centerpiece of my small yard
I jumped in the army jeep on the way to the clinic
Soon we arrived for our rotations
That day I recall a thirty-feet wide migration of song birds
Rolling snake-like over the school, lasting for more than five minutes,
Headed north

We drove back to Ciudad Granja later that afternoon
As I turned the corner I looked at the fence, astonished
The leaf-cutting ants were carrying the last of my beautiful
Passion flowers down into their colony
The fence held only the woody vine
The passion flowers and leaves were gone
I did miss these beautiful flowers
But was stunned at the remarkable passion
Of the ants' labor

## AUTUMN #25

Leaf litter saturated in equatorial sunbeams
Warblers riding south on moonbeams
Persephone's sadness at first frost
Bears dreaming of winter's sleep
Shrill northwestern winds loosening yellow and red
From the sugar maples
Mushrooms exploding in strange shapes
Celebrating All Hallows Eve
Billions of small creatures composting leaves to humus
Late fall snows coax nuthatches, chickadees, cardinals,
And juncos back to the feeder.

Grey skies swallow blue
As pallets of snow sit on the landscape
Freezing mornings blow smoke from breath
And ice small ponds.
The groundhog's hole is dug deeper
Under the barn.
The snow fences are placed
In a clearing as a white tailed ten point buck
Snorts, pounds his hoof,
As if to defy the coming winter.

## DYLAN TAPE

Bob Dylan recorded a song
At a friend's house
It was a tale of Mexican
Migrant workers, the wetback
Caught between two countries
One poor the other rich
A magnet pulling the impoverished
Toward money and education
A desert mirage with resulting catastrophe
He runs the gauntlet
Across the border
Facing arrest
Walking through
The searing heat
Of the Sonoran Desert
Dancing with death

The Zapopan Street Committee
Welcomes Juan and his tape
To the Saturday fiesta
We are all celebrating Juan,
A local rock star
The tequila and mescal
Has been passed between us
There are tacos, chocolate and
Cake on the table
Piñatas hang from the ceiling
There is dance, guitar and song
The Allmans, Eagles, and Jimmy Cliff
Are on the turntable
Juan arrives to the celebration
He looks downcast

The party is over
The tent falls on the circus
He informs us regretfully
That Juan's recorder chewed the tape
The song was ruined
It was never heard,
Like an unfinished symphony
The day was no more than disappointment
With an empty space
Where the Dylan song
Should have been

## GUNSLINGER

Grandpa owned an Army-Navy store
A lion who could easily outflank
His three salesmen
Anxious as gazelles sniffing the air
For predators
A hundred dollars a week
Was their salary
Closing time he'd lock the doors
Cross the railroad tracks
Negotiate the gates
And then drop the proceeds
In the black slot at the bank
Compulsive in routine
He'd pull up his mahogany chair
With red embroidered seat
In front of the TV
Highball in left hand
Cigar in the right
Mirroring the gunslingers
Sitting inside the screen at the bar
Till the westerns killed themselves
Off the air

## HE SMELLED EXOTIC SPICES

He smelled exotic spices which made him dizzy
After he awoke he felt like metal probes
Were exploring his brain
Through the dead space of empty thoughts
The clinging of machines was constant
The pink boulder was growing larger
More time was spent at the liquor store
Guests were rarely invited
Everything he had touched
Seemed like it had been a dream
Those that loved him brought tears
To the memories of yesterdays
Each dream was a prophecy
That gave meaning to the absurd
The power tools of creation were shutting down
The boulder was growing cancer
Spiraling out of control
Though it hung above his queen size bed
As if life stayed forever the same
Though he was constantly changing
Colors in his dreams

# THE MAXIMS

## THE SENTENCE AND THE PERIOD

The sentence was like a battering ram
He liked to charge straight away
As if there was nothing before him
This led to no shortage of complications
Often he would bust right through the period
Obliterating the beginning of the next sentence
Absolutely splintering it into the illogical

The period tried to coach the sentence to slow down
And actually stop before proceeding toward
A yellow and red traffic light up ahead
That would let all meaning pass in time
The impulsive sentence was frequently
Arguing with the period
He just couldn't accept that such a small dot
Could exert such control over him

Wasn't he the agent of meaning?
The stuff from which great novels are born?
The period exclaimed that he was only trying to instill order
For there to be meaning,
There must be regulation
Or all significance could be distorted
After repeated destruction of its structure
The sentence began to respect the period
 Leading to an explosive growth in science and literature

MAXIM
Refusing to negotiate hatches chaos

## THE EARTHWORM AND THE GROUNDHOG

The earthworm and the groundhog
Were both expert diggers
Soil would be gobbled up
And pass right through the earthworm
The groundhog was an excavator
He tunneled by using his sharp claws
To throw the earth to the side and in back of him

They decided on a bright sunny day to have a contest
To determine who could dig the deepest
They would dig within a short distance of each other
To keep track of their positions
The contest commenced with great fanfare and expectation
They dug expertly; the soil was damp.
They descended quickly, tunneling for what seemed like hours
Both were exhausted.

In their haste for victory they didn't realize
That due to the wetness of the soil
Both their tunnels had collapsed behind them
Since they were far underground,
The pressure on the soil in the tunnel had increased
Going back would be like digging through a slab of wood
There was little oxygen and unfortunately
They lost track of the direction they were digging
They dug deeper instead of toward the surface,
Leading to their demise

MAXIM
The journey forward may be as perilous as the journey back

## THE HAWK AND THE FARMBOY

There was a red tail hawk who took up residence in the field tree
The tree was located in the middle of a golden-hewed field
The higher branches of the tree were naked
The bark had been stripped off them by insects, woodpeckers,
And the erosive forces of nature

The hawk sat in the high branches
Spending most of the daylight spying for mice and other delicious morsels
He was quite comfortable spending his days walking up and down branches
Then bouncing from one side of the tree to the other
Always looking for any small movement which might expose his dinner

A passing white tail deer looked up through the branches
Inquiring how successful the hunting was on this sunny day
The hawk began squawking at the deer chasing him from his hunting ground
So he might concentrate on his rodents

Now there was a boy who lived in the farm house on the far side of the field
The hawk did not know that he had seven notches in his wooden sling-shot,
Picking off small sparrows and pigeons that were common visitors to the farm
As the boy walked along the fence line, he looked up into the tree and saw
the Hawk.  The hawk paid little attention, focusing only on the creatures
Running around the base of the field tree

He picked up a small rock
Placing it in the leather pocket of the sling
He pulled the sling back in one swift motion
The hawk, looking toward the ground,
Was struck in the chest, a mortal blow,
Falling from his perch,
As the rodents scattered at the base of the field tree

MAXIM
One must never be so focused on one endeavor
As to lose sight of the imminent risk before him

## THE PORCUPINE AND THE GADFLY

The porcupine was a very serious animal
He spent most of his time hanging from his tail
From a hickory tree in deep meditation
Some of small forest creatures squirrels and chipmunks
Were chattering about a contest that was to be held in one
week

There would be a one hundred dollar purse
For the winner of a five mile race
Time went by and in the end there were two
That would vie for the trophy
The gadfly who looked much like a horsefly
And the porcupine
The porcupine was an unlikely entrant
He was not known for his speed
Although his concentration was excellent
He ran as if he were plodding through mud


Most of the big money was on the gadfly,
The clear favorite
Whose racing skills were unquestioned
On Saturday the contestants were lined up at the starting line
As the gun sounded
The porcupine began trudging down the road
His back undulating like a lizard
The gadfly stayed back on the starting line
Deeply involved in a lively conversation
He was jabbering laughing and having the best of times

Now the porcupine had gained much ground
The gadfly flew swiftly a few hundred yards
And then spied an acquaintance
Whom he spoke with for over an hour

Laughing howling and forgetting himself

The porcupine had run tirelessly
And now focused on the finish line
Just a few hundred yards away
The gadfly was still talking
Splitting his guts in laughter
At the jokes that were traded
By the time he recalled
That he was a competitor in the race
The porcupine was already holding
The silver trophy over his head
An unlikely winner

MAXIM
One must focus on the finish line or he will lose sight of the
course he must follow.

## THE RAVEN AND THE VULTURE

The vulture was circling the field on the same track
For fifteen or twenty minutes
This messenger of death was closing in
Shortening the diameter of each circling
Until the space closed quickly over a raven
Knocked off his feet to the ground
By the vulture's force

The raven took two steps and then sounded
Caw caw, bobbing his head
The vulture was sucking in air
Blowing up his chest, towering
Over the shiny black trickster
Who was daring the vulture to venture forward?

The raven had been toying with a field mouse,
Throwing it up in the air
And then catching it in his beak
The patient vulture stood waiting
For the raven to crush the mouse
He would then move in quickly
Snatching the silent still mouse
From the raven's beak

The raven was not through; he juggled the prey,
Then kicked it as a football
Laughing as the mouse scampered into its burrow
The vulture was exasperated
The rodent's smell was all about
Teasing the vulture's senses
The small field mouse was shivering
With fear but spared for the moment

The hungry vulture was angry

Duped by this sleight of hand
He flew away as the black rascal laughed
He had called death in and with cunning deceived him
The vulture had flown away hungry
Though the raven was in hopping distance of his next meal

MAXIM
New alliances must not be mistaken for greater security.

## THE ROSE AND THE FEVERFEW

The rose grew not far from the feverfew
They looked each other over,
Sizing each other up like two prize fighters
The red rose stood in her full beauty
Her fragrance pulsating,
Drawing attention from the entire garden

The feverfew was similar to a daisy, with white petals
Surrounding a yellow pollen-laden center
The odor of the feverfew was pungent,
Making all the other flowers feel uncomfortable
Sometimes the others would feel sick to their stomachs
If the wind blew in their direction

The rose was the queen; all flowers bowed before her
They would catch her eye, trying to win her hand
The feverfew was generally ignored
Many in the garden just wished it would go away,
Plucked out as a weed or die a premature death

Though the rose's beauty was the center of attention,
Her existence was challenged
There were the aphids of mid-summer,
Drawn to the rose as a magnet
Biting and ripping at her exquisite petals
Then there were the nauseating powders and sprays
That the owners used that seemed to choke the breath from her

The feverfew, because of his foul smell,
Had no difficulty controlling insects
The rose was jealous of the plain looking feverfew
Willing to give away a bit of her beauty
For peace from the constantly attacking aphids

MAXIM
Beauty attracts not only suitors but malefactors.

## THE SKUNK AND THE DUCK

A pond duck befriended a skunk
The duck became fascinated by the black and white skunk
Who would frequently drink at the ponds edge
He swam over introducing himself
Asking the skunk if he wanted to picnic with him
They sat on the long grass between the water
And the edge of the forest
The duck brought several small minnows
The skunk a container of assorted bugs and beetles
They had a grand time eating and talking of their daily exploits
The duck bragging that he could swim ten times around the pond
The skunk that he had the capacity
To scare the fiercest beasts of the forest
The mountain lion and the wolf
Just by moving toward them,

He'd have them running toward the hills
The duck not particularly knowledgeable of his new friend
Was dubious of his boasts
He began prodding the skunk with verbal jabs
Then the foolish duck began nipping playfully at the skunks back
The skunk did not like this at all
He became more disturbed about
The duck's aggressive ill-mannered behavior
He turned his body away
Doing a hand-stand on his two front paws
Spraying the duck with his foul-smelling liquids
The duck waddled quickly back to the pond
Spending the next month trying to free
Himself from the deadening odor

MAXIM
Do not push yourself on an acquaintance too quickly without
knowing his true character.

## THE WILDEBEEST AND THE LION

The lion lived on the edge of the wildebeest's herd
He was an incredible specimen
With his healthy long mane that encircled his head
That held two intense eyes that spied back and forth
Across the Serengeti Plain
The wildebeest lived on the savannah protecting her young
Under constant threat of the lions and other large cats

It was the great migration
The lions followed the wildebeest north
Picking off all the weak old and vulnerable
It was a steady food source for the large cats for months
This wildebeest, a large female, felt that if she could cross the river
There might be freedom from this terrible threat
Ready to take her at any time

She was short on weapons that might protect her
But her plan might work if the lion became over confident
She had run with her calf within a mile of the Mara River
She would find a narrow portion that could be crossed easily
She galloped down a steep incline splashing into the river
Avoiding the crocodiles climbing the ravine face on the other side

The lion was very hungry thinking of his empty stomach
He spied his prey on the far shore
He dove into the Mara ignoring the threat of the crocodile
He was quickly taken to the bottom
By two large crocodiles that had been unobserved
Just beneath the surface.

MAXIM
Though the query is in sight there may be unexpected risks

### BLINDNESS ON THE ROAD

Sara looked back into the forest toward the darkness, inside which she felt safest. The squirrels and chipmunks were foraging for early fall seeds and nuts. A porcupine waddled over the forest floor, quills warning the other forest denizens to stay clear. An opossum was hanging by his tail from a pine bough.

The world was silent but for the engines revving as the cars climbed or descended the hilly back roads. As Alice approached the road she looked down the highway seeing Tanya lying flat on the road. The accident may have occurred as the moon was drenching white light over the deer herd that began to cavort, dancing in the shadows. The road seemed to disappear; the deer forgetting the nature of the cars.

Tommy leapt to the night's rhythms, underestimating the speed of the metal bodies rolling down the road. He went down. His brother became angered, wanting to smash the side of the cars. The automobiles were a mystery with their rude behaviors. The deer could not fight those beings that hypnotized them with their bright penetrating eyes. They stood motionless; turning to statues that would lose their shape after the autos drove through them.

There was a conference called of all the forest creatures, who were upset by the carnage wrought by the metal boxes. They argued, hissed, squealed, and shouted at one another before reaching a consensus. To succeed they must stay off the back roads at all costs and avoid looking into the metal monster's eyes.

MAXIM
There are roads so bright that one becomes blind to the risks.

### MAGNIFICENT SPECIMENS

They grazed in a field lush with green grass traversed by a winding cool stream. The large Black Angus bulls were ambling before each other, showing off their muscular shoulders and chests. They swept their large heads through the grass, chewing out all its various nutrients.

There had been ample rain. The meadow was verdant and thick with grasses. The lushness of the late spring followed a particularly snowy winter. This year was spectacular. The cows dropped many calves that frolicked mindlessly in the pasture, suckling from their mothers' milk, half drunken with delight, crashing into the large bulls, who pushed the calves gently away with their large heads.

It was paradise. The bulls and cows spoke of the wonder of this particular year. And somehow it seemed different, never ending in its rich food supplies and sunny days. The cattle laughed, ran, and grew fat and muscular on their steady diet of hay and fresh grasses which constantly renewed them.

The bulls bragged to the cows that this was the year that they would stay because they appeared so magnificent to their owners. How would they be able to part with such spectacular creatures? But sadly to all the cattle the huge eighteen-wheelers came and took them away as they had done every year before.

MAXIM
Be cautious when attempting to guess the intentions of the powerful and the significance they might impute to their inferiors.

## FROGS ASCENDENCE

The frogs in the king's pond multiplied
That year like a blessing from God
The royalty of the Peeper family celebrated their fertility
This was a forty-year occurrence
The pond was rippling at all levels with these strange creatures
They were jumping on the edges of the pond
Squeezing their bodies through the surface
Like fish gliding on their tails over the water

There were pollywogs in early stages of metamorphosis
With big heads and small tails
Trumpets were sounding through the kingdom
The song was deafening from the pond
A singing most beautiful in four-part harmonies
It was a bountiful time for the Peepers

People came far and wide to hear
And experience their exotic peeping
They stood mesmerized and entranced
By their numbers and the quality of the song
Then as quickly as this happiness bloomed
The frogs began to mysteriously die
Some felt it might have been related
To the finite and dwindling food supply
The Peepers in their great numbers
Had gobbled up all the nutrients in the pond
There was a great sadness that descended
Over the frog kingdom

MAXIM
There must be caution in pronouncing a blessing too hastily.

## CHIPMUNK'S CHATTER

There was a chipmunk well known in his sector of the forest
If a neighboring squirrel or opossum would pass
He would chatter without pause
His friends would avoid his tree taking the long way around
Just to avoid his endless utterances
There was no substance or news just a series of vacant sounds
It was as if he just enjoyed listening to his own chatter
When others tried to get a word in edge wise
It would feel like they were up to their necks in babble
The chipmunk seemed to have no idea of the bad impression
He was making on his forest friends

One day a red-tail hawk landed in his tall pine tree
His head darted quickly spying one object and then the next
The hawk was puzzled when he heard the constant chatter
Coming from a lower bough
It began to make him very angry
The sounds were an insidious overture
That shut out all other sounds
He could not hear the sweet spring voice
Of the nuthatches chickadees cardinals
And orioles

The harmonious melodies of the thrush drove him deep in reverie
The hawk was hungry when suddenly he located
The noisome beast in the lower branches
He flew stealthily to a neighboring redwood
Then flew toward the object of his irritation
The chipmunk was still chattering in the talons of the large hawk
The hawk was not listening
He was only preoccupied with finding a large branch to enjoy his next meal

MAXIM
People don't want an individual around who chatters much and says little.

## THE OVERZEALOUS MEN AND THE WISEMEN

The bureaucrats had collaborated many months
Professing complete transparency in their decision
To send the convict to the prison
The chief officer felt if he was at this facility
He could save them thousands of dollars
Many thought that the convict belonged in a specialized home

He would often scratch his arms, or grab other inmates
He misunderstood the staff's intentions
When assisting him while he brushed his teeth
When the bureaucrats visited
Several in our organization informed them
Of their vast experience with such patients
Extemporizing exactly how one might approach
Such a difficult individual

The officials from the state
Looked slyly at each other during the orientation meetings
As staff gave them examples of their brilliance
Confirming that this was exactly the facility that could meet their needs
They later spoke with the executive leaders of the prison
Complimenting the superb ideas they had described
In rehabilitating this prisoner

They soon promised to send an endless stream of individuals
For rehabilitation

MAXIM
Be cautious of the consequences before bragging to superiors of one's
miraculous remedies.

# THE TALES

### CEPHALOPODS

My father was a marine biologist. In a large aquarium in the basement there was a tank that held ten thousand gallons of salt water. This was filtrated by an advanced exchange system that maximally ensured the cephalopods' safety. I was ten year old when I first encountered these creatures; brown in coloration though could quickly change color to adapt to their surroundings. The octopi had no trouble changing from brown to red, blue, green, gold, orange, and black. They had large eyes.

They looked at me with the same curiosity as I looked at them. Just as a child can learn a foreign language quickly I was able to learn the secrets of their language concealed in their almost instantaneous changes in color patterns. At first I was able to understand just a word or two, but before long I could differentiate subjects, predicates, adverbial phrases, direct and indirect objects. I could decipher the emotive force in their thinking.

It became clear whether a sentence was a statement, question, interrogative or exclamation. In short order something magical happened. I was able to communicate with them as I would my father. At the same time I learned their color-based language. Thereafter the octopi became more than bizarre eight-tentacle large eyed curiosities. Now they were sentient beings that could speak and understand me as I could speak and understand them.

Alice was female; Philip male. Sometimes they would have spats with each other and the aquarium would ignite with color. They could be as understanding or as mean-spirited as any other person. They were like surrogate parents for many years that they inhabited the basement. They would discuss their personal history but were no help in discussions of world history. They had a surprising facility with mathematics. Philip would frequently tutor me in algebra or calculus. He would scold me when I was unable to grasp a concept quickly. On the other hand he was patient, explaining in a clear manner the most difficult problems as one might understand them.

Alice would intervene if I had problems with my peers. If I was at logger-heads with my parents she would talk me through it in a way that was non-threatening. Her coaching in my early years gave me great resiliency for dealing with the most difficult individuals.

I had a girlfriend, Aletha, very cute, smart but controlling. Alice felt I was building a prison around myself to maintain autonomy. But at the same time was losing Aletha. She felt I had to discuss that part of me that needed to be free which in turn might bring us closer. With Alice's assistance, in no time, there was less battling, our relationship grew closer.

Alice and Philip were like other close relatives. We enjoyed spending time together. My parents would think it strange that I spent so much time with the octopi. I never disclosed our mutual language ability to my parents. I thought they would consider me crazy. I did publish a paper on inter-species communication many years later.

Scientists had done research in the past on chimps, crows, and dolphins. All had memory for simple commands and problem-solving. But there had never been any evidence of inter-species cephalopod communication. In other words, grasping another species' language. I was able to communicate with the octopi as a speaker of English and as a speaker of Spanish who could both completely understand each other's speech.

I wrote a book "Color Coding Speech in Octopus and Cuttlefish". The New York Times wrote that "close encounters of the third kind" were within reach in the oceans of the earth. My father taught me everything he knew regarding the homeostasis of the octopi environment in the aquariums. I later worked cooperatively, with input from other scientists, including Mr. Eduardo Rodriguez, a curator of the New York City and Carracas, Venezuela aquariums. My parents died as a result of a small plane accident when I was twenty-five years old. Alice and

Philip became surrogate parents. The octopi lived much longer than the usual life cycle of these creatures; I felt this may have been related to the deep affection and understanding we had for each other.

There was another experience that I must share with the reader. I began to dream in flashing color patterns, translating to octopi speech. I felt that somehow I was caught in the middle of the subconscious of Alice and Philip. I would see the vacillating colors that would translate into English sentences such as "I will evade the moray eel and codfish, I will discharge my ink propelling myself from danger," then more color patterns: "you will always be in our heart, we love you." It seemed that my dreams were their dreams. They both lived to a ripe old age of thirty years. I arranged for both of them to have marble tomb stones in the family plot at Forest Hills Cemetery. Both were then cremated as was their wish. Their ashes scattered over the Pacific Ocean.

## *JOHN RAMSEY*

John Ramsey married Marsha when he was 22 years old. He had been a good student, voted most popular in his class at Benton High School. He met Marsha his senior year at Benton. John was a pitcher who starred in the state high school all star team. His family was middle-class; his dad was a Buick salesman at a Benton dealership. Both Marsha and John decided that college was important. John graduated in four years at State College. Thereafter he earned his CPA degree in Accounting. He then worked as an Accountant for approximately 30 years. Marsha managed the daily challenges on the home front; such as transporting her two children to activities, grocery shopping, bookkeeping and managing the social calendar. John enjoyed coaching the community little league baseball team.

Life was uneventful, just the usual bumps and bruises until John was 50 years old. Suddenly, it was as if a window shattered in their lives. He was accused by a neighbor of exposing his genitals in front of their children. Their immediate friends were shocked; it was astonishing, simply out of character for this individual. He was as straight as an arrow; church every Sunday, with a firm value system. He would always coach his children that you are only as pure as your deeds which serve as God's guide on judgment day. He was arrested, taken downtown to be booked at the Benton Police Station. His family and partners could not believe this – it was a puzzle that begged a solution. He was interrogated, bailed out, returned home where his behaviors were usual. He was unassuming and apologetic to Marsha and his children.

John was a hulk of a man; six foot four, confident, self-assured. He was poised, graceful, carrying his frame effortlessly. Marsha tried to come to terms with her husband's behavior. This idiosyncratic act did not make sense in any way, on any level to her. He returned to work but he felt that people were watching him. The female secretaries treated him differently. He recalled zipping down his trousers. I wasn't doing anything wrong; I had to pee. It was dusk, the sun was setting. The children were at the end of the property. I knocked at the door. Marge didn't come right away. It was beginning to sprinkle; her children were running about. They were not looking at me, I was waiting for Marge. She was going to give me something for Marsha. The kids were staring at me. I tried not to but I caught their eyes. I turned toward them holding my organ; I was shaking it as Marge opened the door. She screamed. I was embarrassed. The kids were laughing and screaming. Everything was in slow motion. I did not mean this. I did not mean this. The thing was set in motion as if I was standing there but not in the movie. It was a black-out, a blank spot. A skipped page in the novel I never read. It was a de-je-vu, like a half-reflection of an event about to happen. My thoughts are racing one ahead of another. They are being shattered, like a window hit with a baseball. The strings are out of tune. There is no forward or backwards to my thinking. Words are flying all over but I'm not using them correctly. The kids are there in the yard, she opens the door, she sees me holding my penis, and I know it's in my hand. The kids are screaming, why don't I move, put it away, nothing's happening. My heart is beating hard in my chest. This is wrong. I'm not supposed to be here like this. Marge doesn't understand, I can't explain this to myself. I can't explain this, what was this?

Marsha asked for a meeting with John's partners. They discerned nothing out of the ordinary. He seemed to be doing an exemplary job. He had a gift for facts and figures. This seemed like it was preserved. But the public relations for the firm was damaged. The partners felt under increasing pressure to do something; if they did not they would risk reputation and business. John was placed on administrative leave indefinitely. His self-esteem was ravaged; like being hit by ten of his fast balls in the chest. He felt like there was an increasing blackness that blurred his understanding of events that were twisting and turning in his mind.

Marge and her husband were good friends with the Ramsey's. They pressed no charges; they dismissed the act as a mistake of ugly coincidences. John was given a six month probation and twenty-four hours of community service. He returned to his work in three months; he was welcomed back with open arms. John smiled across the table; his partners in the firm, George, Pete, and Jim were supportive. They knew John like a brother and were ready to give a fallen friend a second chance. They had all been childhood friends.

As much as loyalty generates comradeship, comradeship stands on competency, every member of a group must perform. A weak partner can't last long in a pressure-cooker of a high powered group. Reputations rise and fall based on high quality performance. Within a month John himself felt strange feelings, waves of anxiety that he couldn't explain. He was confounded by the difficulty he was having with the computations that in the past had been as easy as pitching the next pitch. He found himself referring to his books more. It was as if instead of secure storage banks of memory, he was experiencing unaccountable leakage. Pete and George were the first to notice this change. John would ask for assistence of relatively straightforward accounting problems. He was frequently referred by his partners to source books or crib sheets with formulas. John felt like he was floating off behind; his memory, like car exhaust evaporating in the air.

There was increasing tremor in his hands; his confidence was fading. "I don't drink; the sun is frying my brain. One and one is two; two and two is four; two, four, six, eight; eenie-meenie, eenie-meenie; who is God? Where is he now? I feel lost in a cave. I don't have a flashlight. Mind is lost; what is the cost? Formulas – what is a formula? Where is my mind? Where did it go? Who grabbed my formulas? Words and numbers are not working; they are not fucking working!"

He confided to Marsha that work was not going well. He didn't think he could last long there if things didn't change fast. Now Marsha noticed the changes. He seemed to look right through her as if she didn't exist. He began blurting strange responses to Marsha's questions. "I'm not here; you can't see me. Where am I? I'm not here. Disappearing, disappearing. Love you. Someday, someday, return. You know me. Who am I? Love you. You know I'm asleep. My thinker is broken, Marsha, my thinker is broken. My light is flickering, can't turn it on."

John's children thought there was something terribly wrong. Their dad was changing, molting before their eyes. His movements seemed rigid; his thoughts unclear, at times not making sense. Marsha made an appointment with a psychologist. He completed a battery of test including MMPI, Stanford Binet, personality inventories and a mini mental status exam. The psychologist noted that his IQ was now low average, not what one would expect who had been a member of a high caliber accounting firm. There were profound problems manipulating information and problem solving. Dr. Barnes, the psychologist, referred him to a neuropsychiatrist who ordered an MRI brain scan.

He found what he had suspected - significant atrophy of brain matter in the frontal and temporal regions of the brain. John was not able to speak competently in public; organizing his thoughts internally became a challenge. "I'm a screwball. Why can't I find the kitchen, the kitchen? I want a soda, mouth dry. My head is dry. Where's Marsha? Where are my babies? I can't speak; words don't come out of my mouth. Talk does not seem to make sense. Ideas fade in and out; I can't say them. I can't get what they are saying to me. Nothing makes nothing. Nothing makes sense. Where do I go? I am not safe. They are trying to shut me up. I am not living. I can't read, I can't write. What is happening? What does it mean? I am dying. Life... death. A scythe at the door; death at the door."

His concentration was fractured like the brain tissue his faculty depended on. He no longer recognized his children; he frequently asked who they were. Marsha's overarching thought was to protect the man she loved and that other caretakers respected her wishes. He began to be incontinent of his urine and his stool. In a period of one year, Marsha felt that she could no longer care for him at home. She couldn't watch him for twenty-four hours. He was becoming a risk to himself. John would leave home; the family became frantic unable to locate him. Police were frequently called at first. Marsha soon secured the car keys. Eventually she sought placement in a skilled nursing facility. He would continue to put his arms around Marsha, telling her by his gestures that he loved her. But at other times became crude, groping her private areas in public. As his speech deserted him, his emotions supplanted his rationality. Through much of his day he was terribly frightened. There was intense loneliness; he was receding at the speed of light to the far reaches of his universe, becoming part of dark matter.

At intervals there might be a memory, a fragment somewhat familiar, but the context was terribly blurred. The disease had knocked out the processing centers of the frontal lobe that provide organizational skills. The temporal lobe, the site of memory, was selectively atrophied and resulted in severe impairment of recall. He lost the ability to differentiate appropriate social behaviors. He was eventually hospitalized in a psychiatric facility and died within two years of the onset of his illness. His functioning brain stripped like a Mercedes gutted on the inside for spare parts by this dementia that relentlessly stole his thoughts and humanity. His early indiscretions were now forgiven, seen as a small part of a larger more devastating picture.

## THE WOODEN BOX

The room was hot, stifling in humidity. I asked her if she wanted some tequila. She declined saying "I feel too rotten in this heat to drink." I couldn't understand her point of view. She said she'd rather wait until tomorrow when she could drink in the sunlight.

I have a habit of surfing the Internet while talking with my son. I frequently ask for a clarification: "What did you say?" He'd catch me red-handed multi-tasking. He then laughs at me. I lamely reply that I was listening but missed the last line. It is embarrassing to be caught multi-tasking, a crime of ignorance, blowing off the people you love by losing grip on the last line. "It is a tale, told by an idiot, full of sound and fury, signifying nothing." What if Shakespeare wasn't listening, forgetting his self-talk?

I remember her lying naked on the bed. It is funny in that I'd be drawn to her when I was stuck in self-loathing. Every night when I was a kid my father locked me in a box. It was a wooden box with shelves for books, a closet, bathroom, and an aquarium with fresh-water tropical fish. I would hear nothing from the outside. There was an upright lamp that provided illumination. The air was fresh; I didn't have to worry about the self consciousness of new eyes on me.

I felt free of trying to please. In the morning upon walking out of the box I felt well-rested, completely self-assured as I stepped out into my school day. My homework was finished. I focused on mathematics, physics, the romance languages and history. They seemed to spin through each other magnifying their interest toward me. The girls allured me with their budding youthful rhythms and the magic of their smiles, while at the same time their song and jabber confused me.

The days felt no more real than the night, locked tightly in the box. I didn't ask my father why; I felt no imperative to fight his guidance. I was completely immersed in my books, lost in the behaviors of the zebra, angel and catfish. At first there was never a sense of confinement or loneliness; though I regretted not spending more time with my sister and brothers. I really didn't miss them. We had the weekend and the hours before bedtime.

Soon I noticed messages posted inside the box. I called them mind stimulants. What is a cell? How is ancient Rome similar to New York City? I did see similarities between the box and parallel universes. I thought for sure other boxes existed in the world like mine. I never composed answers to the questions, though they did light my mind. I wondered what my dad's agenda was as I grew older. Was he trying to turn me to his point of view? Or was he threatened that I'd become contaminated by the outside world?

Then I started thinking that maybe he wanted complete hegemony over everything that might influence me. Surely he could control attractions to friendship. It was a while before I considered that he kept me as some sort of experiment. I feared a laboratory assistant would enter the box in a white coat clipping my arms and legs, pinning me in a case like a large Costa Rican beetle.

I think of us lying out in the sun on blankets in the sand and breeze, watching the iguanas and frigate birds, lost in our streams of consciousness. It was then that we broke open a bottle of tequila. She had a smile on her face. We began to look at each other without scorn or remorse. She was pretty, the sun adding sheen to her long dark hair. Her legs long, soft, calling to me.

I'm just awakening in the box. The day is in front of me. I wait for the click on the lock. I want to rush out into the light; a tidal wave impacting the whole world. When will the locking and unlocking stop? As if I agreed to these arrangements with the contract tilted in my father's direction. I grow uncertain that my father will open the box in the morning. His intentions seem less clear; his motives more ambiguous. Why would he want to lock me in this box? I used to joke with my father that I hoped his plans included both of us, but now it seems I am only a model he is building. I'm not sure how much longer I want to cooperate with this box-existence. I feel if he precedes with his plan we may both be harmed equally.

I'm walking the beach with Rita. She draws my thoughts away from themselves. It is maddening that I can't grow comfortable in her company. We smile though I never feel part of it. I think of insurrection. The box grows smaller and I grow larger. I felt my father losing control. I still answer his strange questions. He is constantly evaluating me. This is excruciating. I feel frozen. He can only talk about his stock market successes. At the same time I know he is thinking of his concubines. His conversation leaves me numb. He empties my mind of content. I am fearful of his power. He sucks up my memory, replacing it with his to make me tractable. I start to tantrum in the box. I howl and scream at my impotence like a husky dog baying at the moon. Though blind to the forces outside the box my father locks me away at night.

Rita asks me why I asked her to come to the Tropic of Capricorn to stay with me. This was a question the box couldn't help me with. The frozenness possessed me. At times I couldn't move my left arm in her presence. I felt the pain in my heart going dead. The box taught me discipline and convention. It did not free me of the rigidities and neurosis.

She stood next to me so beautiful. An image of me jumping naked into a frozen Adirondack Lake became a repeated loop as she glances at my body, laughs at my self-consciousness, and then dives after me. I was not comfortable until I broke the surface of the icy water. Like my father unlocking the box morning after morning.

We are walking down the beach in Puerto Vallarta. The sun is later morning, the sands white, growing warm. The sea, blue, undulating with breakers. We take our clothes off; people stare. We drink tequila from the bottle. She is at peace. I am taking a pile driver, smashing the side of the wooden box. I won't live there any longer. My father's cold and imperious. He will have difficulty understanding my anarchy. I set some small quantity of rare earth metals free opening the palm of my hand. The son is free from the father's chains. Rita and I run toward the sea, smashing the blue surf, running up the sunlight.

## CARMEN

Neal introduced me to Carmen. She lived in an apartment she shared with Neal's girlfriend. We felt comfortable with each other immediately. We enjoyed each other's company, drinking, playing cards, dancing and listening to music. Her breasts were ample, filling her halter-top. She wore her short shorts tight, attention immediately drawn to her butt. Carmen had a cute face, pretty smile, and looked her twenty-two years.

Carmen was a serious student. She kept up with her academic schedule while enjoying partying. She'd always remind me to relax feeling I was too introspective, accusing me of being too serious. I couldn't smile enough for her. We would play gin and go out to watch foreign films. She was Puerto Rican raised by her grandparents after her parents were killed in an auto accident. We were on a social service assignment in the country. Their health care was basic. We were joined by a more experienced intern who was part of our team. Treating spider bites, infections and dysentery. When we weren't on assignment we'd spend time riding around in Carmen's yellow taxi. It was large enough that we could lay in the backseat without being seen. Our friendship grew closer. We enjoyed a few glasses of tequila and partying the nights away.

Carmen had a natural rhythm, moving in perfect harmony with the music. Her torso gyrated in concert with her hips. Movements alluring and hypnotic. Sometimes I'd forget where I was when I watched her. My eyes would tangle with hers; both of us lost in the twilight. Carmen would purr "baby" - this would reverberate in my gut, reeling me in for the night.

We drove back to the city's traffic jams, buses, cars, horns, in dissonance. She did not want to return to her apartment. It was Friday. We decided to spend the night at my house: a two floor flat on the outskirts of the city. In the morning we laid in bed for awhile, got dressed, had eggs for breakfast and ended up in the living room listening to the radio.

We had a couple of drinks, she talked about former boyfriends. Carmen loved to increase my jealousy quotient, knowing it would only ignite my passion for her. Using reverse psychology she would say "you don't pay any attention to me, Jimmy, you don't love me."

Then she'd stand in the middle of the room and she'd begin moving her hips in a slow gyrating motion. She knew she had me then. Her rhythm like a horn section with Congo drums, drawing me in. it was a sexy, enticing gravity that pulled men toward her. Her brown eyes glistened, her lips moist and full. She had a deviant smile that slowly grew on her face. We were both anxious to do some shopping. I was enticed, looking at her in her tight jeans.

It was a dry, hot day. Cars and buses were stirring up the dust in the road in front of my house. You could hear horses, roosters and campesinos laughing and singing as we walked out toward the taxi. We both were feeling good walking down a side street, the air was fresh. She looked good in the sunlight. My head was still dancing in the tequila. She said again, "you don't love me baby." We both laughed. Carmen suggested going to a jewelry store in Chapilita. We both knew it well, located in a posh residential neighborhood, not far from Minerva Circle. They had a nice selection of silver, gold, platinum and fine gems: emeralds, rubies, and diamonds. On the way over we spoke of our relationship, the coincidences in our lives. We both had two brothers and a sister; we were both Leos. Both of us wanted to go to medical school since we were in high school. We both enjoyed each other's company: partying, drinking, feeling quite at ease. Again she said "you don't love me baby". I knew she was baiting me. We drove up to the jewelry store at about two-thirty. The sun was high in the sky. We walked through the door, down a staircase into the main floor of the store. Carmen walked to the far back of the shop. I followed her, glancing at the contents of the glass cases. There were fifteen to twenty cases. At first I didn't notice that there were quite a few customers mulling around, just looking, particularly those cases with gold chains, bracelets, and rings. The gold looked exceptionally rich with the case lights directed to the jewelry. An owner came over offering to assist me. I really wanted a thick gold chain. They were priced reasonably but too expensive as far as I was concerned. I walked to the front of the store intrigued by the cases of diamonds. There were gold earrings and necklaces with groupings of diamonds, rubies and emeralds. Everything sparkled in their exotic settings.

I lost myself in the beauty of the jewelry and at the same time lost track of Carmen. I noticed the owners behaving in a peculiar manner, staring furtively over the parameter of the shop. At the same time I heard an alarm. I looked around and saw the managers escorting Carmen to the front of the store. Shortly after I was requested to join her. The owners were perturbed. They pointed to a gold ring that lay on the counter. I was perplexed but it quickly became clear, particularly after I noticed the police walking down the stairs.

They questioned me as if I was an accomplice; both of us were accused of stealing the expensive gold ring. I responded immediately that this was crazy. I looked at Carmen. She said "I did it for you baby". I became enraged. I told the owners who accused me of working with her on this heist that this was mad. I had no idea that she was planning to do this. I could picture my future in a dark Central American prison.

I apologized to the owners for Carmen's behavior. They had a conference with the police that lasted several minutes. They were extremely unhappy, though fortunately, in the end, agreed to drop all charges. The eyes of all the customers seemed upon us. The police were angry; they began pushing at us, using expletives to humiliate us in front of all of those who were watching us. We walked up the stairs into the light.

I was in a state of denial. This just couldn't have happened. There she was standing in front of me, trying to explain the incident away by intimating that it was just her good deed for the day. We got in the taxi; she drove me back to the flat. We had a couple shots of tequila. She repeated her mantra "I did it for you baby; I wanted to get you something nice." I replied that you almost bought me a couple of years in a Mexican slammer. She looked away. At that moment, both of us knew that our time had run its course. It was clear to me that she did it for herself and almost dragged me down into her pit. She walked out the door, I followed her. She sat in the front seat, turned the key and headed for the highway. We never saw each other again.

## WALL OF LEARNING

The academy is a Romanesque cylindrical tower shooting through the clouds in the Italian countryside. The exterior looks like a piece of carved ivory. There is mystery associated with the the history of the Wall of Learning. The jealous call it deception, others find it ethereal, designating the Wall as a wonder of Romanesque architecture. Every two years a student is admitted after passing a series of stringent examinations. Each day of his education the student must ascend to the highest floors possible. There is a stone ramp butting against the inside wall, spiraling up toward the 30th floor. There is an outside rail to protect one from falling. The wall is a touch-sensitive computer- like screen that interacts with the student. It serves as a reservoir recording the highest accomplishments of the scholar.

The walls mark achievements in mathematics, humanities, science, the arts, invention and technology. The student adds his narrative, past, present, and future typing information onto the screen, integrating his insight and adding his personal embellishments into the Wall of Learning. The wall is in perpetual motion. The higher he climbs; the visual tapestry becomes more complex a metric reflecting energy spent in application to his studies. He becomes transfixed on each image. He is inspired by science and literature. As he journeys closer to the upper floors he is enveloped in calmness.

He imputs formulas, memoirs, history and a short story on the wall. He feels part of a great tradition. The tower begins to spin as he becomes weary. The student is filled with tension as he glimpses problems that will challenge his future. He begins running down the spiral ramp, looking back at the walls. They churn like a writhing ocean. His mentors look down upon his achievements. He will begin his quest again in the morning. Each day is less daunting; the learning more exhilarating. In two years he will graduate to the next tower.

## THE STACKER

Eddie worked at the mill like his dad before him.
In the fifties it was a fabric mill.
Now it was a three-floor department store
With an assortment of clothing, electronics, sports equipment
and a food court
Eddie was a stacker; he'd break open the cardboard boxes
Stacking the merchandise in its proper place
Suzie and Ron, high school buddies, were now co-workers.
Eddie's outlook gradually changed.
The boxes of merchandise became boxes of melancholy.
He confided to his friends his overarching sadness toward the
daily drudgery.
More boxes, endless stacking
Stacks of boxes to the sky like New York City skyscrapers

The sadness grabbed him; it shook his foundations.
Taking him down a pit that had no bottom
Soon he was hospitalized at a psychiatric unit,
Given antidepressants and electroshock treatments.
Eddie's center post was twisted.
Suzie and Ron had visions of Frankenstein being jolted with
massive bolts of electricity.
They pleaded with Eddie to stop the treatments,
Telling him that he might shut down or his brain might burn up
He neglected his buddies; their pleadings seemed pathetic and
unkind. At times he awoke from dreams, his brain writhing and
screaming

As time passed he had visions of returning to the mill
Surprised that as he stacked he became most at peace
He achieved serenity as he stacked his seven and a half hour day
He ignored all that was going on around him;
Questions from customers, the din of the mill,
The frantic pace of his environment

No longer was his life only bleak, with boxes piled so high,
Each box was now a point of starlight with exotic origins

The stacker's life was solitary; it's meaning a mystery
His friends at the mill thought of him
Frequently catching his dreams
Ron often visited him at the hospital
Where he sat in a straight back chair
Between his single bed and wooden desk
He often wore a faint smile on his face
Looking through the small vertical window with metal bars
Silent but for the motions of his hands and arms
As if he were stacking at the mill

www.ingramcontent.com/pod-product-compliance
Lightning Source LLC
Chambersburg PA
CBHW032048040426
42449CB00007B/1030